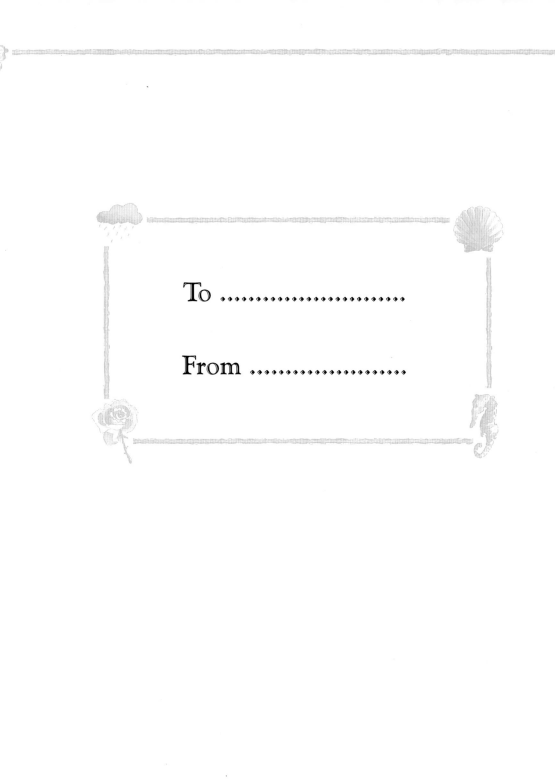

To ....

From ....

To my children
Luke, Sophie,
Lily, and Grace,
whose prayers of faith
and expectation have fed
me and encouraged my
own journey of faith.

A Child's Book of Prayers

Written and compiled by

Glenda Trist

TYNDALE HOUSE PUBLISHERS, INC.
Wheaton, Illinois

A DORLING KINDERSLEY BOOK

Commissioning Editor Elrose Hunter
Project Editor Shaila Awan
Senior Art Editor Diane Thistlethwaite
US Editor Constance Robinson
Illustrations Carol Hill
Production Josie Alabaster
Picture Research Anna Grapes
Jacket Design Simon Oon

This edition published in the United States by
Tyndale House Publishers, Inc.
351 Executive Drive
Carol Stream, Illinois 60188

2 4 6 8 10 9 7 5 3 1

Visit Tyndale's exciting Web site at www.tyndale.com

Published in Great Britain by Dorling Kindersley Limited

ISBN 0-8423-1973-5

Color reproduction by GRB Editrice S.r.l., Verona, Italy
Printed and bound in Italy by L.E.G.O.

Contents

"Prayer is conversation with God"

CLEMENT OF ALEXANDRIA

Prayer is, quite simply, the way our hearts
turn toward God to listen and respond
to him. As adults, we may need to regain
a childlike approach to prayer,
but children are naturally spontaneous,
and tend easily toward trust and faith.
There is much we can learn from a
young child about prayer!

Prayer in daily life

Recognizing that children are naturally open to prayer,
what can we do to encourage and develop their lifelong pursuit of it?
We can create an environment for our child where prayer becomes a
spontaneous, daily part of life. Prayer can be presented as an enjoyable
conversation with someone we love and trust. Prayers of praise and
thanksgiving are preferable, since these come naturally and easily
to children. We can help our child turn happy events and small joys
into prayers. Simple needs or concerns that arise in our child can
also be turned into prayers: sick pets, lost toys, skinned knees.
Our child's own walk of faith has begun, and ours
is strengthened as we experience prayer together.

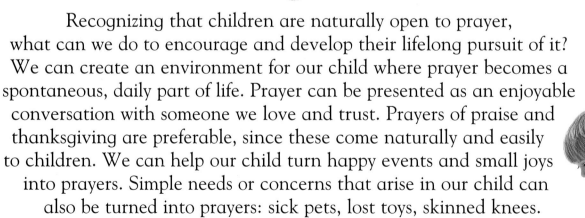

Teaching a child to pray

This book is a collection of short, simple prayers designed
to help your child develop an awareness of God.
Share these simple prayers with your child, and enjoy a
special time of love together.

The prayer that Jesus taught us

Our Father in heaven,
hallowed be your name,
your kingdom come,
your will be done, on earth as in heaven.
Give us today our daily bread.
Forgive us our sins
as we forgive those who sin against us.
Lead us not into temptation,
but deliver us from evil.
For the kingdom, the power, and the glory are yours,
now and for ever.
Amen.

Prayers
about
my feelings

Sometimes we feel happy because we had a good time. Then it's good to say thank you to God. At other times we may feel lonely, angry, or sorry. God wants us to tell him about those feelings, too.

I smile when I am happy

I smile when I am happy.
I scream when I am scared.
I frown when I am jealous.
I cry when I am sad.
Thank you, God, for all
these feelings, good or bad.
Amen. Lily

I will praise you, O Lord

I will praise you, O Lord,
with all my heart;
I will tell of all your wonders.
I will be glad and rejoice in you;
I will sing praise to your name,
O Most High.
Amen.
PSALM 9:1–2 NIV

I played computer games today

Dear Jesus,
I played computer games today.
I had such a great time!
I played really well and got my highest score ever.
It was fast and I had to think and move fast.
But I did it!
Thank you so much for my computer.
Amen.

We had the giggles today!

Dear God,
We had the giggles today!
There were so many funny things
to laugh at with each other.
And we were doing
lots of silly things,
such as funny faces, silly rhymes,
and jumping on the beds.
Thank you for a fun time!
Love from me.
Amen.

When I am quiet

Dear God,
When I am quiet
I sit by myself
and think about how
you are all around me.
And that makes me feel happy.
Amen.
Grace

Please help me not to feel grouchy

Dear Jesus,
Please help me not to feel grouchy
because it makes me feel bad.
Amen.
Bolu

You made the thunder

Dear God,
You made the thunder.
It's just like when I'm angry.
You made things just like our feelings.
So you know how I feel.
Help me not to be angry.
Amen.
Grace

It's not fair!

Dear God,
It's not fair!
And I'm really, really upset.
And I don't like my mom and my sister!
And I wish they'd go away.
I don't really.
But I needed to say that to someone.
Thanks for listening, God.
Amen.

I don't think anybody loves me today

Dear Jesus,
I don't think anybody loves me today.
Everybody's grumpy and grouchy.
But you're not.
You love me and make me feel special. Always.
I'm glad I'm your friend today.
Amen.

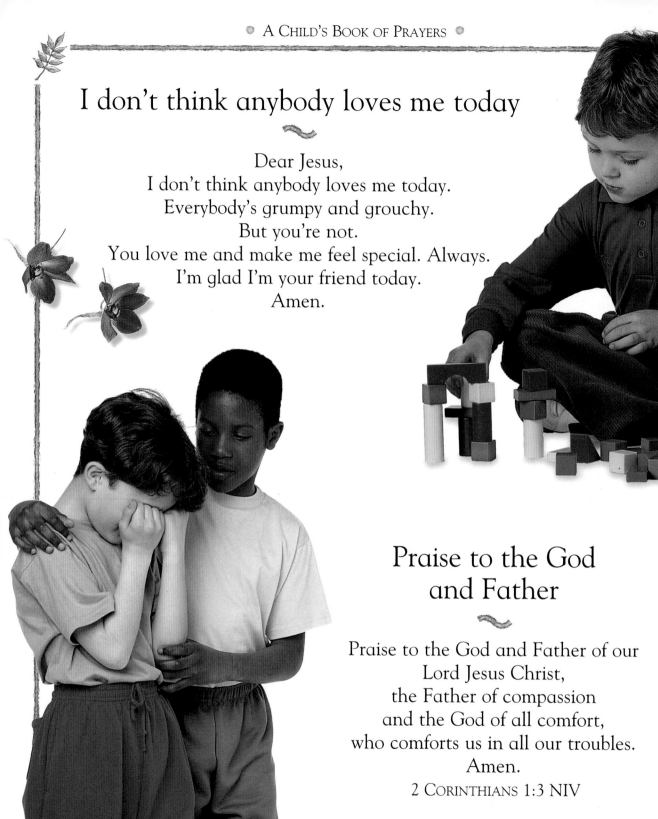

Praise to the God and Father

Praise to the God and Father of our
Lord Jesus Christ,
the Father of compassion
and the God of all comfort,
who comforts us in all our troubles.
Amen.

2 CORINTHIANS 1:3 NIV

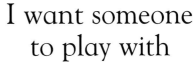

I want someone to play with

Dear Jesus,
I want someone to play with.
But everyone else already
has someone to play with.
Except me.
I feel sad and lonely.
Help me to remember just how much you
love me, Jesus.
Because that makes me feel better,
like I'm not all alone.
Because I know you are my friend.
Amen.

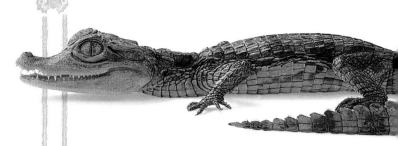

Prayers
about
animals

Animals are a wonderful part of God's creation. They are there for us to enjoy, but God also wants us to look after the animals and protect them.

Lord, you have made so many things!

Lord, you have made
so many things!
How wisely you made them all!
The earth is filled with
your creatures . . .
large and small alike.
All of them depend on you
to give them food when they need it.
You provide food and they
are satisfied.
Amen.
PSALM 104:24–28 GNB

Thank you for making animals

Dear God,
Thank you for making animals
so that we can enjoy them as pets,
or see them in the zoo and in the wild.
Please help people to stop
harming animals.
Amen.
Lindsay

Today I played with my dog

Dear God,
Today I played with my dog.
I had a ball and threw it.
And every time my dog
brought it back for me to throw again.
And it was really slobbery!
I just wanted to thank you for my dog.
We're good friends.
Amen.

You made some pretty strange animals

Dear God,
You made some pretty strange animals.
A kangaroo with huge feet
and a pocket for its baby,
a spider with no neck and
eight legs to trip over,
and fruit bats that can only sleep
upside down hanging on a tree!
I think you are very smart,
but I think you
must also love to laugh!
Me too.
Amen.

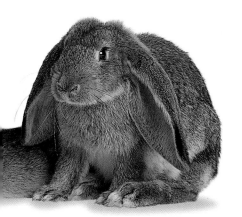

Thank you for our hamster

Dear Lord, thank you for our hamster.
Thank you for making a pet
we can cuddle and stroke.
Thank you for making her cute
and furry and nice to look at.
Please help us take care of her properly.
Amen.
Timmy

Hear and bless your beasts

Dear Father,
Hear and bless
your beasts and singing birds,
and guard with tenderness
small things that have no words.
Amen.
ANON

Prayers about my day

God makes each day brand-new for us. It is great to know that God goes with us through each day and wants us to talk to him about the things we do and the people we share our day with. These things are important to him, too.

Today is a new day

Dear Jesus,
Today is a new day
and I am one day older.
I can do lots for you today!
Help me to be kind and helpful.
Help me to wait my turn and
clean up my things.
Help me to have fun and enjoy
your wonderful world!
Amen.

Thank you for helping me

Dear Jesus,
Thank you for helping me
with my spelling test at school.
I want you to help me always.
With love, Jonathan
Amen.

Thank you for my school

Dear God,
Thank you for my school.
My teachers are nice and
I enjoy school most days.
Amen.

I am learning to read

Dear Jesus,
I am learning to read
and that makes me feel smart.
Thank you for giving me a good brain
and making me smart.
I'm going to like reading.
Amen.

I went on the train today

Dear God,
I went on the train today
and out of the window I could see
all the trees and houses whizzing by.
When you're up in heaven, God,
do you see everything on earth whizzing by
as the world spins around?
Amen.

God be in my head

God be in my head and in my understanding;
God be in my eyes and in my looking;
God be in my mouth and in my speaking;
God be in my heart and in my thinking.
Amen.
MARIA WARE

Thanks for today

Dear God,
Thanks for today,
for being with friends
and for dressing up and
giving concerts and
having fun.
Amen.

Thank you for the day today

Dear God,
Thank you for the day today,
and for my family.
I liked it when I dug up the ants' house
and saw all the ants.
Amen.
Larissa

Thank you for this lovely meal

Dear God,
Thank you for this lovely meal,
and also for the people who made it.
Please help those who don't have food.
In Jesus' name, Amen.
Lily

Thank you for the world so sweet

Thank you for the world so sweet.
Thank you for the food we eat.
Thank you for the birds that sing.
Thank you, God, for everything.
Amen.
E. RUTTER LEATHAM

Prayers at nighttime

Saying good night to Mom and Dad is special for all children. Saying good night to God, our heavenly Father, can be just as important.

When I lie down

When I lie down,
I go to sleep in peace;
you alone, O Lord,
keep me perfectly safe.
PSALM 4:8 GNB

It's time for me to go to bed

Dear Jesus,
It's time for me to go to bed.
But I don't feel safe in the dark.
My mind tells me there are things in the dark –
scary, moving things that I don't like.
Please stay awake when I fall asleep
and protect me from anything that might
hurt me or make me afraid.
Thank you for keeping me safe last night.
Please do the same tonight.
Amen.

Thank you for shiny stars

Dear Jesus,
Thank you for shiny stars at night,
for bedtime stories,
and good night hugs.
Thank you for my warm bed
and quilt to hide under.
Thank you for making me feel
safe and cozy and sleepy.
Good night, Jesus.
Amen.

Prayers
about
my friends

*Friends are precious and we
want to tell Jesus about them.
Jesus is our best friend.
From him we can learn how
to be a good friend to others.*

Thank you, God, for sleep-overs

Thank you, God,
for sleep-overs with a friend.
It's more fun, playing with a friend.
Thank you, God,
for being able to rollerblade with a friend.
I would be lonely without my friends.
Amen.
Alison

You loved me enough

Dear Jesus,
You loved me enough
to die on the cross for me.
Help me to be a friend like you.
Help me to care as much
about my friends as I do about me.
It's hard.
Amen.

Thank you for our friends and family

Thank you for our friends and family.
If we did not have any friends we would be sad and lonely.
Help people not to judge other people by their skin or religion.
Amen.
Lacey

Thank you for my friends

Dear Jesus,
Thank you for my friends.
We have such a good time together.
Every day I can't wait to see them!
Amen.

It's great to be your friend

Dear Jesus,
It's great to be your friend.
I like having you with me every day.
I like talking with you at any time.
Amen.

Jesus, friend of little children

Jesus, friend of little children,
be a friend to me.
Take my hand and ever keep me
close to thee.
Amen.

WALTER JOHN MATTHEWS

I was awful today

Dear God,
I was awful today and called
someone stupid names.
I didn't stop to think how it
would make them feel.
I'm sorry, God.
Please help me to stop
being mean
and to think about others.
Amen.

Breathe on me, breath of God

Breathe on me, breath of God:
fill me with life anew,
that as you love, so I may love
and do what you would do.
Amen.
E. HATCH

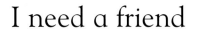

I need a friend

Please Jesus,
I need a friend.
I would be kind and share
and play nicely with her.
Please send me a friend.
Amen.

My friend is sick

Dear God,
My friend is sick
and I don't want him to be sick.
And I know he doesn't want to be sick.
We want to play together.
Please, please, make him better.
Amen.

Most gracious Father

Most gracious Father,
visit this family and household
with thy protection.
Let thy blessing descend and rest
on all who belong to it.
Amen.

JOHN CHARLES RYLE

Prayers
about
my family

*God gives us families
to love and care for us.
We can talk to him about
the tough times and the
great times in our family.*

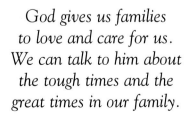

My mom loves me

Dear Jesus,
My mom loves me. My dad loves me.
And my grandma and grandpa love me, too.
My whole family loves me!
Thank you for my family, Jesus.
Thank you for giving us families
to teach us how you care for us.
Amen.

Bless Grandpa today

Please Lord,
Bless Grandpa today and help him to feel better tomorrow.
Please bless all our family today and please help Grandma
when she's looking after Grandpa.
Amen.

Larissa

Was your mom wonderful?

Dear Jesus,
Was your mom wonderful?
Did she smell nice
and did she take good care of you?
My mom does.
And she gives great snuggles
and knows special secrets for us to share.
Thank you for giving us moms!
Amen.

No wonder we are happy in the Lord!

No wonder we are happy in the Lord!
For we are trusting him. We trust his
holy name. Yes, Lord, let your
constant love surround us.
PSALM 33:21–22 SLB

I want to thank you

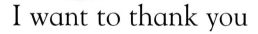

Dear God,
I want to thank you for a very special gift
you have given our family.
My mom just had a baby!
He's really cute and has tiny fingers and toes!
(And now I'm not the baby in the family!)
Amen.

You gave me a great dad

Father God,
You gave me a great dad
here on earth as well.
He can fix almost anything and
can carry me on his shoulders.
I hope I'll be like him one day.
Thank you for my dad.
With love,
Amen.

Please bless Mom

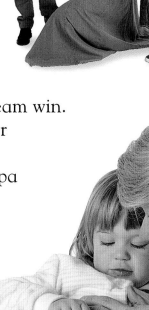

Dear God,
Please bless Mom
and give her time to rest.
Please bless Dad and make his soccer team win.
Please bless my brother and sister
and help us not to fight.
Please bless Grandma and Grandpa
and make them come to visit.
And God bless me and help
me to grow tall fast!
Amen.

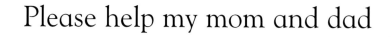

Please help my mom and dad

Dear God,
Please help my mom and dad
get all their jobs done
so they can play with me.
Amen.

Today my mom and dad had a fight

Dear God,
Today my mom and dad had a fight.
They sounded like they really hated each other.
It made me scared.
God, you know I love them both.
Please take care of them and teach them to love
all the good things about each other.
Amen.

It's not fair, God

It's not fair, God,
you were supposed to make
this world a good place!
So why are there brothers?
Stupid idiot brothers.
You just can't expect me to love him!
But I know you do.
Dear God, I'm glad
you are so strong because
I need a lot of help from you
to love someone
I'm very angry with!
Amen.

Our family is really small

Dear God,
Our family is really small.
Just me and Mom.
My mom takes care of me
and goes to work.
She does everything.
I love my mom.
Please take care of her every day.
Amen.

Prayers
about
special days

*There are some days that are
full of good memories – parties,
celebrations, special places to go,
favorite people to be with.*

I'm starting school!

Dear Jesus,
Guess what's happening tomorrow!
I'm starting school!
It's so exciting. I'm a big kid now.
But what if I get lost?
I hope I find a friend.
Please be with me
at school today, Jesus.
Amen.
Sophie

I think every day is special

Dear Jesus,
I think every day is special
because you made it!
Amen.

I love Christmas Day

Dear God,
I love Christmas Day.
It is fun when we open our presents.
Christmas is really about Jesus being born.
Amen.
Ian and Jasmine

This is the day

This is the day which the Lord hath made:
let us rejoice and be glad in it.
For the beloved and most holy child had been given
to us and born for us by the wayside
and hid in a manger because there was
no room in the inn.
Glory to God in the highest
and on earth peace to men of good will.
Amen.
FROM ST. FRANCIS'S VESPERS FOR CHRISTMAS

With shepherds we watch

Dear God,
With shepherds we watch,
with kings we adore,
with angels we sing
praise your son evermore.
Amen.

We are moving today

Dear God,
We are moving today.
I'm going to miss all my friends very, very much.
I hope that I will find new friends at my new house.
I will miss my bedroom too.
But my new house is big and good
for playing hide-and-seek in,
and that will be exciting.
Amen.
Sophie

I love the sea, Jesus

I love the sea, Jesus.
I love the waves that chase me on the wet sand.
I love the shells and making seaweed drawings.
I love the sand and digging holes and burying my legs.
Jesus, I love you even more for making the sea.
Amen.

Easter is really hard to understand

Dear Jesus,
Easter is really hard to understand.
Why was Good Friday good if you died?
Why did you have to die?
Please help me to understand.
I'm glad you came to life again, though.
That I can be happy about!
Amen.

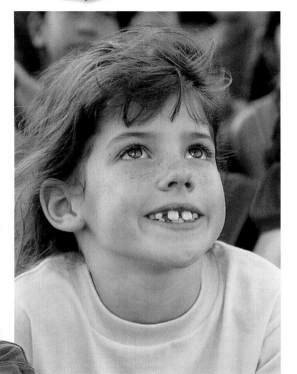

Forgive me, please

Dear Jesus,
Forgive me, please,
for all the wrong or selfish things that I do.
Come into my life and make me brand-new
with the life you had when you came to life
again on Easter Day.
Amen.

Thank you for birthdays

O Lord,
Thank you for birthdays.
Thank you for all the excitement and
fun on birthdays –
for parties and presents and the friends
who bring us presents.
We pray for those who can't have parties or
presents on their birthdays.
We pray that they will still be able to
celebrate their special day.
Amen.
Timmy

I'm so excited

Dear Jesus,
I'm so excited I'm going to have a birthday party
with a special cake and games and balloons.
Thank you, Jesus, thank you!
Please help my friends to have fun, too!
Amen.

Thank you for my birthday

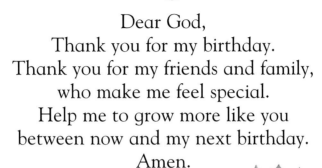

Dear God,
Thank you for my birthday.
Thank you for my friends and family,
who make me feel special.
Help me to grow more like you
between now and my next birthday.
Amen.

Prayers
about
the world

Our world is a big place.
There is so much to see and do.
We can tell God about our delight
in our world and our worries about it.
We know he cares about the world.

You created the day and the night

You created the day and the
night, O God.
You set the sun and the moon
in their places;
you set the limits of the earth,
you made summer and winter.
Amen.

PSALM 74:16–17 GNB

Thank you for the wonderful world

Dear Father,
Thank you for the wonderful world
that you created for us to live in.
Please help us to look after the world
and all the creatures in it.
Amen.
Susanna

Thanks for the great day

Thanks for the great day we had today,
for the sun and playing outside.
I enjoyed the grass and the trees
and those flowers we saw.
I enjoyed lots of things about
the world today, God,
Beautiful things that you made.
Thanks for thinking of us
when you made the world.
Thanks for making things
that we can enjoy each day.
Amen.

We shall have this day only once

Dear Lord Jesus,
We shall have this day only once;
Before it is gone, help us to do all the good we can,
So that today is not a wasted day.
Amen.
STEPHEN GRELLET

Help the people who live on the street

Please God,
Help the people who live on the street
to get a home to live in.
And help them to get clothes to wear and food to eat.
Amen.
Amy

Please stop the wars and fighting

Dear Jesus,
Please stop the wars and fighting.
People are getting hurt.
Children too.
Please give food to the many hungry families
who have no food for tomorrow.
I know you care about these people, too.
Amen.

Help us be honest with each other

Dear God,
Help us be honest with each other and
talk with each other whatever color or religion we are.
Help us make peace around the world
so it can become a friendly place.
Help us share our things and not be greedy.
Amen.
Sophie

Index of prayers

Acknowledgments

Scripture verses on pages 8 and 12 are taken
from the *Holy Bible*, New International Version®,
NIV®. (NIV). Copyright © 1973, 1978, 1984 by
International Bible Society. Used by permission of
Zondervan Publishing House. All rights reserved.

Scripture verses on pages 14, 22, and 44 taken
from the *Good News Bible* (GNB) published by
The Bible Societies/HarperCollins Publishers Ltd.,
© Copyright American Bible Society 1992.
Used with permission.

Scripture verse on page 32 taken from
The Simplified Living Bible (SLB), copyright
© 1990. Used by permission of Tyndale House
Publishers, Inc. All rights reserved.

The publisher would like to thank the following for
their kind permission to reproduce their photographs:
t=top, b=bottom, r=right, l=left, c=center

Pictor International: 13 tl, 22 bl; Tony Stone Images:
Bob Thomas 38 bc, Charles Thatcher 41 tl, Chip Henderson 26 c,
Howard Grey 34 c, Jerome Tisne 10 tr, Jon Riley 20 bl,
Peter Cade 19 c, Tess Codrington 31 tr; **Telegraph Colour
Library**: 9 br, 33 tl, 47 b, Chris Ladd 37 cbl, Denis Boissavy 25 tl,
Dia Max 44 tr, Guillaume Bouzonnet 28 c, Masterfile 45 br.

Additional photography by Paul Bricknell, Jane Burton,
Andy Crawford, Geoff Dann, Jo Foord, Steve Gorton,
Colin Keates, Dave King, Ian O'Leary, Stephen Oliver,
Susanna Price, Tim Ridley, Andrew Robb, Karl Shone,
Steve Shott, Kim Taylor, Jerry Young.